Write Non-Fiction

Blueprint to writing non-fiction eBook that skyrockets your sales

Melissa Johnson

CONTENTS

INTRODUCTION: THE SECRETS OF WRITING A BOOK THAT PROFESSIONAL GHOST WRITERS REFUSE TO REVEAL

We're in the throes of a revolution.

In fact, we're actually in the midst of at least two revolutions. The first one, that of the growth and ease of use of technology, spawned the second in the publishing field.

Today it's easier than ever before to become a published author. The process has never been faster and less expensive to initiate. The risks are far fewer and the potential audience is larger than you could ever imagine by trying to distribute it around your hometown and surrounding areas.

If you listen closely, you can hear the sound of doors opening up throughout the world for those who had always wanted to be novelists. The explosion in the self-publishing market isn't limited to the fiction genre, though. Not by a long shot.

There's never been a better time to be a writer of nonfiction. For that genre, thanks to the same burgeoning technology, is growing exponentially as well. The same truths hold true in this area of self-publishing. It's quick, easy and especially inexpensive.

In fact, this marvelous revolution in the fundamental way books are printed – and read, by the – is making each and every one of us potential authors. Yes, even you can become an author whether you have previous writing experience or not.

Just one word about that promise. I'm not promising that you'll become any award-winning author although you very well may be. What I am saying that by finding one or more niche topics and take some time to develop book ideas and outlines, you'll discover that you can write well enough to write not just one nonfiction book, several books, in several different niche markets. Or perhaps you'll tackle several of these books in a single market.

What can this book do for you? Take you step by step through the process of writing a nonfiction book. But not just any nonfiction. When you're through reading you'll learn the secrets professional ghostwriters use every day to write swiftly without sacrificing quality, succinctly covering all the points necessary and entertainingly without losing the reader's attention or the essence of the message.

But more than that, you'll see that your book sells – at an exciting and quite profitable rate. Yes, you could say your sales will "skyrocket" once you learn even a handful of these secrets. Before you know it, you'll have several books, all of which are collecting royalties for you with every sale.

And now to introduce the final feather in the hat of self-publishing non-fiction books: It doesn't cost you anything --- not one red cent.

This is such an important point allow me to re-emphasize and rephrase it. You risk absolutely no money up front, thanks to the latest "publishing" equipment, the internet and most of all Amazon.com, which has done more to open up the publishing industry since the invention of the Gutenberg press.

What objections do you have to overcome before you'll believe you can author a popular nonfiction book?

Don't know where to start? Not convinced you're talented enough to write a book? Maybe you're thinking that you're not an "expert" in any one topic to explain it to others? And the objections continue.

Well, stop objecting right here and now and keep an open mind. As young as this field is, there are already thousands, if not hundreds of thousands of individuals making full time livings writing nonfiction books and then self-publishing as ebooks. You never, ever have to print a paperback book unless you have a certain demand for it.

Why should you believe me? Because not only am I living proof that you can earn a living range self publishing, but I have nearly decades of experience ghost writing nonfiction books for others – from hardback, to paperback and yes, more ebooks than can even recount.

Along the way, I've learned how to work fast and efficiently and to keep the words flowing in a way the keeps the reader wanting to turn that "electronic page."

How to Use the Book

This book is broken down into seven essential points. As soon as you grasp the first point, then you can move on to the next. Each point builds on the previous one. You may want to read all the essential how to guidelines first and then go back a second time and actually dig into the nuts and bolts of implementing them. When you read them the second time, you can read them a lot slower and actually begin putting your book together.

The first aspect of writing a nonfiction book is how to choose a topic. Even if you know what you're passionate about and know immediately what you want to write about, read this chapter anyway. If you don't, you'll be losing out on valuable insights that may cost you money when it comes down to the sales of your book.

In the following chapters, you'll learn how to organize your ideas through outlining what will become your books table of contents and how to research in the digital age. In the next section, I'll show you not only how to stop staring at that blank page and start writing. This is also the session in which I reveal some of the secrets of the professional writers – some of which reveal how they keep their momentum going when all they really want to do is shut the computer down and watch some television.

Once you get the book written, from introduction to the last chapter you may believe your work is done and you can present it to your audience. Not so! This is the point where you give it that tender loving care in the way of editing and proofreading.

You'll be amazed at how this will make your book shine in the marketplace. But more than that it will label it as a professionally written book. Before you know it, readers will be clamoring for even more books from you.

I'll also reveal some of the best-kept secrets of the writing community, including:

The 20-minute technique. It will get your fingers flying over your computer keyboard for 20 minutes at a time and have you writing at your maximum speed and surprisingly your most fluent and coherent rate.

"Mind-mappng" trick. You'll be able outline your book using this wonderful trick If you're visually oriented you'll find you can outline a book in literally minutes.

Before one word is written, organize yourself. The behind-the scenes tip to getting yourself organized even before you write a single word. You'll be amazed at the amount of time you'll save with this method.

And much, much more!

If you're struggling with a book in progress now, this tutorial volume will help show you where your weaknesses lie. If you have yet to start writing, then this book is just what you need to read before you dive into your new project.

I'd like to ask you one small favor. I'd greatly appreciate it that once you've read this book that you'd take the time to leave a written review at this link:
www.amazon.com
By reviewing it and telling me what advice and suggestions have been most helpful – and what you'd like to see more of – I'll know how to help you become better authors and sell more books. Thank you!

What are you waiting for? That book won't write itself, you know. It'll just seem like it is.

1 KNOW WHAT YOU'RE WRITING: CHOOSING A TOPIC

Someone once said, "Write what you know." It's been repeated so often that people take this as gospel. Because of this, many potentially talented authors never write a book.

"What do I know?" they ask themselves.

And, sadly, they decide they know little, if anything, the general population would like to read. I say sadly because some of these writers (not all of them, mind you) are talented with a distinct voice that would be a valuable contribution to the industry. Yet, the words, "Write what you know" echo in their heads and they believe they aren't born to be nonfiction authors.

Inherent in these paragraphs are two concepts I intend to challenge in this chapter. I'm about to give you free reign to write on any subject you'd like from some battle of the Revolutionary War, UFOs, to conspiracy theories.

Or perhaps you're interest in the topics of organizing the clutter in homes, how to boost self-esteem or any other topic under the sun. It really doesn't matter. I'm about to turn what you thought you knew about choosing a topic upside down. I'm about to challenge the validity of these two concepts: Write what you know and the idea that you don't have a singular contribution to make to the topic of your choice.

Write What you Know? That's Hogwash!

If every person limited themselves to writing only what they know, then there wouldn't be more than a couple million books on Amazon.com right now. There wouldn't be bookstores with expansive selections, magazines on all topics, and articles on the internet that are yours to read with just a flick of the finger. The truth of the matter is the world would be a pretty sad and boring place.

Instead, I tell those interested in writing their first nonfiction book, "Know what you write." Notice how a simple change of placement of two words in that sentence makes all the difference. Instead of restricting and inhibiting you from writing a nonfiction book, you're being given permission to write anything you'd like – as long as you know your topic.

I can hear some people saying right now, "Well, that's just silly!" Others are puzzled scratching their heads asking, "How in the world do I do that?" It's not silly and really quite easy to do. And you can describe the process in a word: research.

What you don't know, you research. With the internet, research has never been easier (as long as you use discretion in selecting your sources). It's your research which will establish you as an expert and authority on the subject. Some people tell me this is cheating. As a history and journalism major in college, the idea of research became second nature to me. You learn by research. What you don't know you reach for a resource to help you understand it all.

What really opened my eyes to this idea was the statistics I heard one nonfiction writer cite. He said that you only had to read five – count 'em five – books on one subject and you would know more than the vast majority of people on that topic.

Think about it. It makes sense. But, inherent in the truth to that statistic is the power of research. It unlocks many doors, opens avenues of inquiry. But more than that, when you research, you have added to your knowledge. Now, you can sit down and write about the topic of your choice. And more importantly, you can feel confident that you're starting out knowing more than many people already.

I'm not saying that you won't need to read more and research more, but now you can be confident that you not only know what you're writing, but indeed, you are writing what you know as well.

Follow your Passion

Do you see how this concept frees you to write on something you may already have a passion for, but not enough "knowledge" of? Are you a collector of antique toys, but never thought you knew enough or were any type of authority to write a book. Think again. If you call your book "A Beginner's Guide to Toy Collecting" or something along those lines, you can help the person who is just dipping his toes in toy collecting to learn a bit more.

And with a little more research in a topic you already love, your book is bound to be excellent. Your book will not only inform the reader, but with any luck your book will ignite a fire within him to pursue this hobby. (And hopefully clamor for more books from you!)

Don't know much about an obscure topic like UFOs but have always been curious about it? Certainly you could find at least five books . . . and countless websites, magazine articles and other information to research. While you're doing this, you're establishing yourself as an authority on the subject.

What if you Don't Have a Passion?

"But what if I don't know what my passion is yet?"

I get asked this quite a bit, especially by younger writers. They could be interested in many different subjects, but can't seem to settle on any one they care enough on which to write.

This is naturally understandable. In fact, I was like that for many years. I hit upon the niche markets that have been my standard writing fare years ago, when I was asked to ghost write nonfiction books. The topics varied, but they all centered about natural health. Before I knew it I was steeped in knowledge. And I was developing a passion for the topic.

If you haven't been fortunate enough to develop a passion, then do what many niche marketers – regardless of the product they're selling. Make a list of topics.

This theory states that the only road to success is by choosing a topic that hasn't been overwritten by other writers. While there's no easy way to do this . . .

Wait there is an easy way and it's called SEOquake. It's an extension to your taskbar that allows you to read a topic's popularity. It also has several other extensions that allow you to measure a topic's popularity within the internet community.

It's not difficult to use. You'll simply type in a topic and the software actually rates the topic and the web sites for you. The higher the number, the more visitors the site has and by extension, the more popular it is.

Another part of the software allows you to type in several topics to discover how many hits they have received in the last month on Google. From there you can use your sense of judgment whether you think you can make a valuable contribution to the topic. When you find a topic through SEOquake that looks like you can write about and be able to market, you still have one more step to take before you can go to the outlining and writing stage of your book.

Can your Book Make a Unique Contribution?

Go to Amazon.com to see how many books are already written on the topic. Don't let this discourage you, however. Regardless of the topic you choose, you'll find something already written on it.

Go through the table of contents or a free sample of a select few of the books to see if you can add something substantially different to the body of literature that already exists. If you can, write it down somewhere in your notes and tuck it away safely for later in the writing process.

You'll also want to read the reviews of the books you're checking out. Don't limit yourself to the good reviews either. See what the readers didn't like about the book and pay special attention to what they think is missing from the book. What did that author not include that the reader wants to read. Write this down. This gives you an even better idea of what your market wants.

For all of the directions, suggestions and tips provided in this chapter, don't dwell too long on this portion of writing a nonfiction book. Find a topic, research it, and get into the meat of the writing. Whether you're following your passion or following a trend in books, you can now be confident that you're off to an excellent start.

If you've found anything in this chapter extraordinarily helpful, please tell me as part of your review of this book at:

www.amazon.com

I personally read each review and seriously consider the suggestions you make. The review you leave is the only method I have of helping you become a faster, more accomplished writer – and help you achieve the stunning success you deserve.

Your next step in the process of writing a book is to organizing your research, your own ideas and making a coherent outline out of it all. While it may sound chaotic, you're about to discover that a little bit of organization goes a long way. Follow me to the second chapter to discover what I'm talking about.

2 ORGANIZING THE JUMBLE: CREATING A COHERENT OUTLINE

Congratulations! You've chosen a topic for your nonfiction book.

Now you have two choices. You can either continue to research the material until you believe you've exhausted all your resources, then outline the mountain of facts. Or – and this is the choice I recommend – based on this preliminary research you can create what I like to call a "tentative working outline." This outline is based It's not meant to be carved in stone yet. In fact, the beauty of this is the freedom you have to tweak it if needed.

If you write many nonfiction books, you'll discover that eventually, the moment you begin your initial research, you'll begin thinking about the order of your outline. Until then the primary research and the outline may cause your head to spin.

Even with this relatively small amount of research in front of you, it may seem as if from where you're standing right now, you'll never be able to capture the most important ideas. But, with just a little bit of time and effort, you're about to discover how easy and near effortlessly it is to take these ideas to the next level and place them in a way that not only makes sense, but will facilitate quick writing.

I'm talking, of course, about the "dreaded" outline. It's at this point that many "would be" authors are separated from the others. These individuals give up on their dream

– and a potentially amazing income that could come from not only this book but future projects as well.

For the longest time, creating an outline was my least favorite part of writing a book. This is because when I was in high school and even college every teacher insisted I turn in an outline before I wrote a paper.

I couldn't do it. I loved it, though, when a teacher or professor allowed us to hand an outline in at the same time I turned in the paper. What made the difference? I would write the paper first and then made an outline. I got quite good at organizing all the material in my head and flowing from topic to topic.

This is not the recommended method of writing an essay let alone a book. So please don't pass over this section believing you don't need it. Outlining really does make writing a book much, much easier to write and saves you so much time.

But I've come to peace with it for many reasons, the biggest of which is a secret I learned and will teach it to you later on in this chapter.

Creating an outline is nothing more than deciding where bits of data, information, statistics and even anecdotes will be placed within the book. There are several ways to do this.

The first way is the method you learned in school. It would look something like this:

How To Write a Non-Fiction Book

1. Introduction
2. Chapter 1: Title

A. Subhead
   I. Point one
   II. Point two
B. Subhead
   I. Point one
   II. Point two
3. Chapter 2: Title
A. Subhead
   1. Point one
   II. Point two

Of course, your chapters may have more than two subheads. But you get the idea. Somehow you separate your ideas and topics then make a decision about where in the book they should be placed.

I find this form of outlining stilted and actually quite unnatural. I've recently discovered another way to get the job done that better suits the way my mind works. This is where "mind-mapping" comes in.

If you've never heard of it, or never have tried it, I recommend that you give it a try with your first nonfiction book. Some people call it a "brain dump" because allows you to get all the information you have about the topic on your book on paper (in any order, by the way) before you begin to actually organize it.

It's a great method of seeing what you have. There are several routes you can take, but the easiest is described below.

1. Simply take out a plain piece of paper, preferably printing paper, but even lined notebook paper works. Turn it on its side so it's horizontal.

2. In the middle of the page either write the temporary title or at the very least, the topic of the book. Either circle this or block it off in a rectangle. Everything else you do from here, in essence, radiates from this point.

3. On the left side of this structure, write the word "Introduction." Every book has an introduction.

4. Now, from left to right put in your various chapters. At this point, you probably have a good idea of the chapters perhaps even some of the names of them. Write out the chapters around this main structure. Box them or circle them and make sure you've connected them to your book's title by drawing a line from the boxed chapter to the main structure. If you know at least the topic of the chapter fill that in too.

You're probably beginning to see a flow chart of sorts forming. That's basically what you have here.

5. Now, with the preliminary research you've already done, working chapter by chapter, create, points that radiant from each chapter you want to include. When you're done, you should have a page that looks something like this:

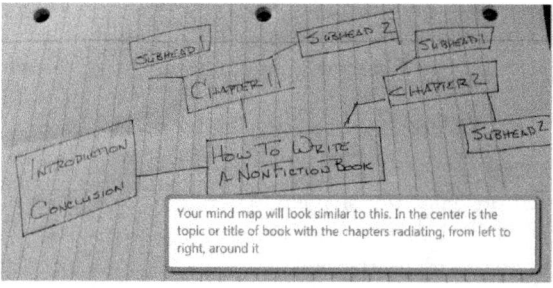

Your mind map will look similar to this. In the center is the topic or title of book with the chapters radiating, from left to right, around it

6. Depending on the size of the book you're writing and the number of facts you plan to put in each chapter, you may want to create a separate mind-map for each chapter.

This is a great idea because it gives you plenty of room on a page to add pertinent details as you come across them. If you recall, at this point you've only done preliminary research on your topic. Sure, you may have read extensively, but you haven't gotten down to the nitty-gritty of digging up your information yet.

You'll also find when you do this, the pages won't seem so cluttered and you'll be able to more quickly identify the points you need to write. Below is a graphic of what a single chapter looks like mind-mapped:

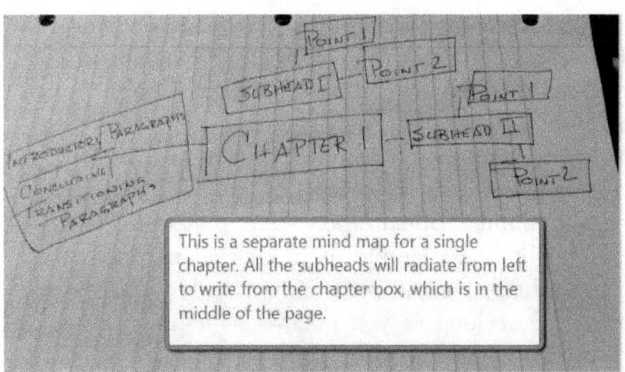

This is a separate mind map for a single chapter. All the subheads will radiate from left to write from the chapter box, which is in the middle of the page.

If you like to create a larger version of this mind-mapping process, you take these very same steps with a large poster board and Post-It notes. Find a place to set up the board and create Post it Notes for the book topic or title and place it in the middle of the board.

For each chapter, create a Post It note to connect back to the book's title. You may want to use different color notes for each level. The color of the Post It note that your book in the middle of the mind map is yellow. Then every note that identifies a chapter could be blue. Then all the subheads that come directly under that you put on notes of yet another color. For example, you may want the middle note to be blue with all the chapter titles on yellow Post It notes.

By the time you've completed this exercise, your mind-mind should be color coded according to levels of organization. That is all chapter headings are one color all subheads are another. If you end up mind mapping in even more detail then all topics under the subheads are another color.

In either case, the concept is the same. It may be that neither of these methods appeals to you. You may have a personal outlining , organization secret that works well for you. It might be as simple of placing all pertinent facts under umbrella code-words that only you would understand. As long as you believe a method works for you – use it.

3 LET'S RESEARCH SOME MORE!

Wait! Before you take this suggestion literally you need to decide how much more research you believe you'll need. If you've never written a nonfiction book before, you may be wondering just how much research you'll need. That would depend on several aspects of your book.

1. You need to set parameters for length.

Search ebooks and print books on Amazon.com. This site always lists the number of pages each book contains. Find a few books on the topic you're writing to find out the number of words those books have. Keep in mind that the standard publishing industry estimation for the number of words on a page is 225.

To get a rough idea of how many words these books are multiply the number of pages by 225. For example, if a book on your subject is 50 pages, you know through this method, that the author wrote approximately 4,000 words.

Once you've decided on the number of words in other books, you can determine what you'd like the length of your own work to be. It may also use this in judging how much data is available for your topic. You may find (on rare occasions) that the research available won't sustain the size of the book you originally thought you could write. In that case you may want to downscale your book. Or, on the flip side, if there is more information than you originally believed, you may want to expand the parameters of it.

2. Be flexible on what you include (or exclude) from the book.

As you continue your research, you may find out you can broaden the contents of your book some. While you don't want to add extraneous material your audience doesn't care about, you may go into a more detailed analysis of a subtopic that will expand the readers' basic understanding of the topic. If you do this, be sure that what you include is related to your main topic.

Expanding your research is especially helpful if you're writing a "how to" book. These are the books that take the reader step by step through a process, whether it's growing roses or making homemade soap. If you could write another 100 words that assure the reader she's proceeding in the right direction then that only enhances your original idea.

On the other hand, if you discover that you're about to go over your intended word count, you may want to scale back on topics that aren't quite as important. You may want to group several subtopics together instead of tackling each one separately. This may mean combining subtopics under a larger umbrella-type subhead. Or it could mean that you combine two or more chapters.

Doing either of these isn't the end of the world, because, remember, you called your outline "tentative" and "working." Now you understand those terms. And when you're working with the mind-map technique of outlining it's easy enough to make these changes.

In any case, now that you have topic, outline and a rough idea of the number of words you're writing, you can begin to research in earnest.

3. Verify. Verify. Verify.

You've undoubtedly already discovered how convenient – no, how essential – the internet is to you, the nonfiction writer. You can find some gems of wisdom and dollops of data that are essential to your explanations.

But, as I have you already realize that not all internet sites are created equal and there are some you just can't trust. It's very important then that before you start throwing statistics in your books, you verify they are correct.

How do you do this? The same way professional journalists are taught to research and investigate before they print or quote anyone. Get a minimum of two sources to say the same thing.

Be sure, though, with the internet that the two sources you find aren't both publishing the same article. You'll notice that many sites run identical articles. Ensure that your information is confirmed by at least two separate sites receiving their information from different sources.

If you can't find another internet site to confirm the information, don't hesitate to look into print books or other sources. You'll also want to make sure that your sources are credible. Facebook, by the way, doesn't count as a source. But definitely make a stop at The New York Times online site for news items, political facts, even historical statistics as well as WebMD if you're writing about medical issues. The Mayo Clinic site is another reliable site for medical information.

With time, you'll develop a host of "go-to" sites which you trust. Keep in mind, though, that even when you have a trusted source, it's best to get a "second opinion."

This same advice is essential when you take information from a print book or if you're interviewing an individual.

Don't for a minute take the doctor's word for something. Make sure that what the doctor or dog breeder is telling you is confirmed by at least one other source.

4. Meet your new best friend: the library

It's true. You're going to discover the rumors that the library is an obsolete place are totally inaccurate. In fact, now more than ever is the time to discover the power of the library's resources.

No you don't have to spend hours within in its walls to determine this either. You're probably well aware of what a library used to look like. Now add things such as computers, ereaders, and all sorts of other resources to that picture.

Plus, if you can't find anything – whether it's a physical book, an obscure fact or you just want to double check a statistic – run, don't walk, to the reference librarian. She or he will either know exactly where and what it is or know how to retrieve it for you. Yeah, librarians are that good. They can save you quite of bit of research time – and they do it cheerfully. Allow them to help you. That's why they're sitting behind that desk.

5. The Personal Interview

Whenever possible you want to add authority and weight to your book. The best way to do this is by interviewing people who work in the field in which you're writing. If you're writing about natural health, seek out a naturopathic doctor to interview. If you're writing about a specific dog breed, like the Japanese chin, find a knowledgeable and reputable breeder.

When you interview them, use every means you can to

ensure you record what they're saying. Don't be shy about taking notes and using a recorder. When it comes time to use this information, then be generous in giving them credit for their contribution. In fact, you may want to quote these persons word for word.

When you do that, you'd write it and place their exact words in quotation marks. Either before or after the quote, you'll *Dr. Smith said,* or *according to Dr. Smith.*

If you find yourself questioning something they said or you don't believe you got the facts straight, then call or email the expert in order to clarify the data. Don't worry about whether she'll be irritated at the interruption in the day or even if he'll view you as incompetent. The bottom line is she'll appreciate your dedication to getting the facts right.

If any of the advice in this chapter or any chapter especially resonates with you, please let me know via a review of this book at:

Similarly, if you'd like to know more about this or any other topic covered in this book, let me know that, too. I'll be sure to consider it for inclusion for an updated version or this book or future books on the subject of writing nonfiction.

It's time, now, to get to the portion of this book you've probably been waiting for the actually writing of it.

4 GETTING STARTED: WRITING THE BOOK

Hear that?

That's the sound of knuckles cracking as people get ready now to write "the book." You sit down at your computer or perhaps you take pen and paper in hand and look at your research.

This is the time you make good use of your mind map if you have one. If not, take out whatever outlining method you use. You're going to consult this outline for two reasons. The first is to calculate the number of words would be appropriate for each chapter, based on your total word count.

Here's what I mean. Below is the example mind map we used earlier. Let's say you've allotted 8,000 words for your book. Most authors try to keep all the chapters relatively the same number of chapters. In this particular book, there are seven (7) chapters. There's also an introduction and conclusion.

I take the number of chapters and then add the introduction and conclusion as an additional chapter. I don't count either of these as full chapters because usually I don't need as many words for these. So, now we have eight (8) segments. At this point you simply divide the number of these segments 8,000 words. This is easy enough to do. Each of your chapters will be approximately 1,000 words.

Take the 1,000 word limit you now have for your introduction and conclusion and divide this by two. You have just given yourself a word limit of 500 for each of these. I discover that usually write more than 500 words for the introduction, but struggle with a coherent conclusion that is of ample length. It may be you'll end up allotting your words differently. After you've written several books, you'll find a style of introduction and conclusion that works for you and you'll know how many words to allot each of these sections.

Keep this upper limit on chapter word count in mind as you write in mind as you write each chapter. If you do this you're far less likely to overwrite on a chapter. Don't worry if go several hundred words

Divide your Word Count Again

You may believe that once you've focused into a chapter you're ready to take off. But, you'd be even more on track if you count the current number of subheads you have under chapter one and divide your chapter word count by that number.

Let's say that chapter one is estimated, according to your word count, to be approximately 1,000 words. You discover you have five (5) subheads under this chapter. This means you divide 1,000 into five segments. Each subhead will be approximately 500 words.

This part isn't written in stone, but by keeping track of this it helps you to know a little better where you are in your word count. You'll know if you're looking at more than your initial, total estimation or if you're coming up short.

Another Jumble of Facts

As you look at your facts, you may be tempted to feel just a touch overwhelmed. This is the second reason you have your mind map by your side. Don't worry. If you just take every subhead under your chapter separately and concentrate on writing on one subhead at a time, you'll be amazed that the book will practically write itself. Take it out and look it over. Your first section of course is the introduction. I'm here to tell you to forget about it! At least for the moment. It's okay. You're off the hook on this one. Most people wait until the book is entirely written before they tackle the introduction.

Onward to Chapter One!

That means your attention goes immediately to chapter one. To get your creative juices flowing, study your mind-map for chapter one. You'll see all of your subheads and many ideas you originally had for the chapter. Take one of these subheads and go through your research and write.

Keep in mind that as you write these various segments, you'll eventually want to have a transitional sentence that naturally guides the reader from one topic to the other. Don't worry about that yet. If your creative juices can't think of a good introductory paragraph, go to the meat of the subtopic.

This may sound even stranger than skipping over the introduction. When you're writing a nonfiction book, it really doesn't matter where you start. You can begin at the start of chapter one or the middle of chapter two – or anywhere else for that matter.

The point I'm trying to make is that you can start where it's the easiest and where you feel the most comfortable. After you start writing, you'll find the words flowing. And before you know it you'll be looking at a chapter on its way to completion. I also guarantee as you find the words flowing to the page, you'll arrive at that introductory paragraph for the chapter as well as an appropriate ending for the chapter which takes your reader seamlessly to the next.

This should be enough to get you started and if you ask any writer, that's half the battle. The other half is maintaining your interest, speed and enthusiasm level in the content.

The next chapter is all about an ingenious secret ghost writers use to help keep their interest regardless of how they feel personally about the subject matter.

5 STAYING INTERESTED: MAINTAINING THE MOMENTUM

Don't feel badly. It happens to even the most seasoned professional ghost writer. What am I referring to? I call it fading interest. Ghost writers are those who write books so their clients can put their own names or a pseudonyms on it. Many times, these professionals don't have a say in choosing the topic.

Eventually, they may find themselves writing slower and slower. At some point, they may even discover that they aimlessly start staring out the window watching the neighborhood children get off the school bus.

There's a simple method that not only gentle guide them writing diligently, but challenges them to write as quickly as possible. I call it the "20-minute monster word workout."

It's actually a series of timed writing sessions in which for 20 minutes your entire focus is on your writing. Of course, the best way to ensure that you have enough material to write for this length of time to have all your topics already organized as we've discussed in the previous chapter.

Have your notes or ideas jotted down so you can flow from one paragraph to another without hesitation.

I'll let you in on a secret. This is probably the best way to ensure your progress, buoy your spirits and keep the creative juices flowing. At the end of your 20-minute workout session count the number of words you've written. Keep track of these either in a notebook or somewhere, because at the end of three sessions, you may want check to see how many words you write in a minute.

In order that you don't experience writer's burn out too quickly be sure to take at least a five-minute break between every writing session. It's essential to your health, by the way, if after three continuous writing sessions you abandon your computer and walk around the house, yard or office for five minutes or so. When you return to it, you'll discover yourself refreshed and ready to start another 20-minute workout. Once you return, you may even find your creativity enhanced. Many writers do.

But what if you do all of this and you still can't keep your interest? Good question. Then perhaps it's time to work on another project for 20 minutes or so. Don't close out the book you're working on. Keep the document open and in front of you because you'll want to go back to it shortly.

For the moment, though, do what you have to do keep your mind off it. You may want it in another 20 minutes when you return to it with fresh eyes and mind. On the other hand, it may be time for lunch, another cup of coffee or even a quick trip to the fitness center. Try out various scenarios to discover which ones work well for you. It may be that at one time or another all of these will work.

When you Retire Writing for the Day

If none of these works, it may be time to take a natural break for the day. Even Hemmingway had his limits on what he wrote in a day. This world-renowned writer had a trick of his own, though, when he closed his "office" for the day. He arranged it so that when he returned the following day he could jump right in with writing where he left off. There was no trying to decide where he was or what should happen next.

Yes, I know you're writing nonfiction and not a Pulitzer Prize-winning novel. It doesn't matter. The aim is to make it as easy on yourself as possible to return to your writing quickly the following day.

You can do this. Ensure that you have your research lined up or even a few words of notes to jog your memory about what you had planned next.

Creating a Sacred Writing Space and Time

Another way writers ensure they write as quickly as possible is to set a "sacred time" and "sacred space" for their writing. Some even have a set ritual. At the end of performing this rite every morning, the writer's body and mind know that it's time to settle down to work.

One of my friends who makes a living writing has developed an excellent morning ritual. She wakes up, starts a pot of coffee, performs a short set of Pilate exercises, and even meditates before writing. Once her meditation is finished she pours herself a cup of coffee, sits down at her computer and spends her time writing. By the way, she's a habitual user of the "20-minute monster mileage word count." She swears this gets her geared up both intellectually and emotionally for her writing.

Do you already have a morning ritual you could adjust to signal its time to write? If you don't, think of an activity or a short series of activities you can do to get yourself moving. Some writers go out to the garden to weed and tend to your flowers or herbs. Others actually get out of the house and go to the local coffeeshop where they drink some coffee, perhaps peruse the daily paper or have a quick pastry.

I have a friend who works the morning crossword puzzle before he gets down to work every day. One puzzle. That's it. Then he's ready to dive into writing. Some writers even take out notebooks first thing in the morning with their first cup of coffee and just start writing whatever comes to mind. They write three to four pages as quickly as they can without regard to content, spelling or even correct grammar. They just write.

These are just a very few of the tips professional ghost writers use in order to maintain focus on their projects. If you can create a few of these that you believe would work for you, use them. It may very well be you already have a ritual to fuel your adrenaline for writing. If you do, make it work for you.

If you can think of other, similar, rituals to get your keys moving on the keyboard or your pen working on the paper, try them. If the first one doesn't work well after several tries, don't hesitate to move on to another which holds promise.

One day, sooner than you think, you'll find yourself practicing something that moves your writing forward every day.

If you have any suggestions on how I can help you become a better, faster writer let me know by leaving a review of this book at the following link:

I'm always interested in helping writers become published authors.

6 The Indispensable Post Script: Editing, and Proofreading

One day, you'll discover you're finishing up the conclusion of your book.

Hooray! Pat yourself on the back. But don't believe your work is ready to be published. Sorry to be the person to burst your bubble. You're so close to being done it's unbelievable.

So what more do I have to do?

You're about to differentiate your book from the vast majority self-published tomes on the market today. You're going to take the time to comb through it, proofread it for typos and accuracy and edit it for grammar mistakes or essential clarifications.

Is There a Difference Between an Editor and Proofreader?

Before we consider the options, let's consider the role of an editor and proofreader. While many individuals consider these activities as one job, they are separate activities and are very often assigned to two individuals.

However, just as often a good editor will also proofread your material. An individual trained in proofreading may not be capable of editing your material.

You can expect an editor to offer suggestions to rewrite certain portions of the text in order to clarify issues. It may be your editor will suggest that specific sections be expanded. A good editor will give you the option of you rewriting this copy or she may offer to rewrite herself.

An editor will also catch any copy that contradicts something written elsewhere in the book. What many would-be authors don't realize is that when a professional publisher accepts a manuscript the book eventually goes through several layers of editing before it's released. Don't view the editing process as an optional step in the building your book. It's absolutely vitally essential.

If your editor doesn't proofread . . . she's not a bad editor. Many writers hire a separate proofreader simply to catch all the misspellings and grammatical errors. Be sure, whatever option listed below that you use, you clarify the scope of the project.

There are two ways you can do this. You can either do it yourself, enlist the help of friends and family, or you can hire a professional editor and proofreader to do it.

You probably aren't surprised to learn that there are advantages and disadvantages to each option.

Planning on Editing Your Own Work?

Watch out. It's here you'll learn how difficult it is to edit and proofread your own material. I'm not saying it can't be done, but it's not easy. You'll have to keep a keen eye on your manuscript and scrutinize the words carefully.

As you read through your book, you'll soon discover that your mind sees exactly what it expects to see, regardless of what's on the page. This may mean that in editing you may miss major issues that a second set of eyes would find.

The other problem is that you know your topic forwards and backwards. You may believe you've explained an issue fully only because you've worked with it for so long. But that doesn't mean your reader will totally understand it.

If you do decide to go with this option, put your own personal feelings about not only the content, but also the writing itself. Many writers refuse to cut words out of their books because they think their words are so unbelievably well written. If you decide to edit your own book, be sure that you can critically review and cut words if necessary.

There are Two Other Options

The first is that you enlist the help of family and friends; the second is to hire a professional editor and proofreader. Obviously, there are pros and cons to both selections.

Let's say you're considering hiring a close friend. Below are some of the disadvantages of this choice:

1. Are you sure your friend will read your book critically?

Choose a friend that can honestly tell you when your writing needs revision without you taking offense. You may have many friends who would be perfectly suited for this job. If you choose one be sure it's an individual who won't injure your feelings when they criticize it. Personally, I only have one friend I would trust this job to. She's the only person who can tell me when something isn't working and I wouldn't take offense.

Ensure that the friend will read it critically. You don't

need someone to read it over once and tell you how wonderful it is. Well, we all need that, but that

shouldn't be your editor. The job of an editor is to carefully – and in this case impartially – read the copy for improvement.

2. Ensure your friend that regardless of her edits your friendship is stable.

A friend may fear that if she criticizes your work, it may damage your friendship. If you do hire a friend qualified to edit your work, reassure her that your friendship will remain intact regardless of what she thinks of your work. Then, keep your end of that bargain.

3. Make sure your friend is qualified to edit a book.

Here's something I've learned: everyone who reads believes she can write. By extension, everyone who reads believes they can also edit. If you truly believe your friend will not improve your book, just say no. Then find another source.

Before you allow anyone to review your book critically ensure that they are qualified.

The Third Option: Hiring an Editor

The final option is to hire a professional to edit your book. Many self-publishers, in fact, do this. And many are pleased with the final product. But you should realize that this will cost money. How much money depends on the length of the book, the experience of the editor and the nature of the edits.

Some editors won't even quote a price until they see the extensiveness of the changes they need to deal with.

Of course, the more work they feel is involved into bringing it up to professional publishing standards, the more they'll charge you.

How an editor establishes his price varies widely from professional to professional. Some charge by the hour; others price by the word. Still others will just provide you an estimate based on the scope of the project itself.

To get a feel for what some editors charge, go to the following page: http://www.the-efa.org/res/rates.php. It's part of the Editorial Freelancers Association site. It provides you with standard rates.

You may be able to find good editors who charge reasonable rates on such sites as elance.com, guru.com and odesk.com. Those individuals, such as yourself, who are in search of freelance help place the job they have on the site. Individuals present their qualifications and the price they'd charge for the project as described. The person who's posting the job, can then select a freelancer, based on quality of work, price and delivery time.

This may not be an option that is within your budget at this time. But it's one I highly recommend when you can afford it. You'll be amazed at how the quality of your book improves when it's touched by a professional editor.

Guess What Happens Now?

Now congratulations are due! You've completed writing your nonfiction book. Take a moment to bask in the sunshine of your success. You deserve that much. You've done everything on the editorial side to ensure that your book will be eagerly read by the hundreds of thousands.

Conclusion: The Start of a Brand, New Career

Once you've written your first book using the methods outline in these chapters, the easier you can then transfer them to the construction of your next book. By the way, that book, too, will generate sales beyond your wildest dreams.

Not only that, but you'll discover the actual writing of the second book will flow much more quickly when you follow the basic steps we've already put into practice:

1. Choose a topic and research it until you feel confident enough to write about it. You now know more about this topic, according to some sources, than 95 percent of the population.

2. Create a table of contents (often abbreviated TOC) based on your research as well as the table of contents of other books you've found on the topic.

3. From this create an outline that follows your table of contents, but detail it a little more fully.

4. If you feel the need, this is the time to do a little more research to fill in any questions or concerns you may have.

5. Begin writing with your outline in front of you to keep you on point. This can be the most intimidating part, staring at a blank document. For this reason, start anywhere. Start with what interests you most or what you feel is easiest to write about. You can write introductory paragraphs to chapters later as well as transitional sentences to gracefully slide you from one subhead to the next.

6. Keep your momentum rolling by using the 20-minute

writing tracker. You can shorten or lengthen this time period that you write nonstop. The point is that by timing yourself, you're immersing yourself in the moment. You're focused in that short period on your writing and the topic and nothing else.

7. Edit, proofread and edit again if you must. Then let it go. Once you feel you've done all you can to make it professional. Send it on its way. Far too many would-be authors get caught up in this web of editing, end up second-guessing themselves and never publish. Don't make this mistake.

Do all of this and by the time you've finished you have an income-generating runaway hit book! Your readers will discover it fast. And before you know it you're creating your second book – using these same trusted methods.

When you've finished with the second book your readers will find that one even quicker and you'll discover that you are gathering an even larger base of fans. Why? Because if you've done your job right (and I suspect you have) you'll already have a base of fans eager for your second book and eager to share the news with their friends.

Congratulations! You're closer than ever before to becoming a published author. There's really nothing stopping you now.

Now that you've finished reading this volume, would you please take a moment of your time (I know you're busy diving into researching and writing that book) to tell me how it has help you. You can leave your review at this site: www.amazon.com.

If there are any topics you'd like to see covered in this book or future publications, let me know that too. This book has one purpose and only one purpose: to awaken the writer within. I appreciate your reading the book.

www.ingramcontent.com/pod-product-compliance
Lightning Source LLC
Chambersburg PA
CBHW071019180526

45168CB00003B/1489